George H Pettis

Frontier service during the rebellion; or, a History of

Company K

First Infantry, California Volunteers

George H Pettis

Frontier service during the rebellion; or, a History of Company K
First Infantry, California Volunteers

ISBN/EAN: 9783337211745

Printed in Europe, USA, Canada, Australia, Japan

Cover: Foto ©ninafisch / pixelio.de

More available books at **www.hansebooks.com**

PERSONAL NARRATIVES

OF EVENTS IN THE

WAR OF THE REBELLION,

BEING PAPERS READ BEFORE THE

RHODE ISLAND SOLDIERS AND SAILORS

HISTORICAL SOCIETY.

THIRD SERIES — No. 14.

PROVIDENCE:
PUBLISHED BY THE SOCIETY
1885.

FRONTIER SERVICE DURING THE REBELLION;

OR, A

HISTORY OF COMPANY K,

FIRST INFANTRY, CALIFORNIA VOLUNTEERS.

BY

GEORGE H. PETTIS,

[Brevet Captain United States Volunteers; Late First Lieutenant Company K,
First California Infantry, and First Lieutenant and
Adjutant First New Mexico Infantry.]

PROVIDENCE:
PUBLISHED BY THE SOCIETY.
1885.

FRONTIER SERVICE DURING THE REBELLION.

THE first battle of Bull Run had been fought. The government had become satisfied that the slaveholder's rebellion was not to be put down with seventy-five thousand men. The Union people of the United States now fully realized that the rebels were to use every effort on their part towards the establishment of the Confederacy, and the men of the north, on their part, were ready to "mutally pledge to each other our lives, our fortunes, and our sacred honor" to preserve the government as their fathers before them had pledged themselves to establish it. The loyal States were ready to respond to any demand made upon them by the government, and there were none more anxious to do their duty to the old flag than the Union men of California.

The people of that far distant part of our country were, in the early days of our "late unpleasantness," stirred to their very depths. A large portion of the inhabitants had emigrated from the southern States, and were, therefore, in sympathy with their brethren at home. General Joe Johnston was in command of the military department, and a majority of the regular officers under him were sympathizers with the rebellion, as were a majority of the State officers. The United States gunboat "Wyoming," lying in the harbor of San Francisco in the early part of '61, was officered by open advocates of secession, and only by the secret coming of General E. V. Sumner, who arrived by steamer one fine morning in the early part of '61, totally unknown and unannounced, and presenting himself at the army headquarters on Washington street, San Francisco, without delay, with, "Is this Gen. Johnston?" "Yes, sir." "I am General E. V Sumner, United States Army, and do now relieve you of the command of this department," at the same time delivering the orders to this effect from the War Department at Washington, were the people of the Pacific States saved from a contest which would have been more bitter, more fierce, and more unrelenting than was exhibited in any part of the United States during all those long four years of the war.

As I have said before, the prompt and secret action of the government and that gallant old soldier, General E. V. Sumner (for you all will remember that California had no railroads and telegraphs in those days), prevented civil war there. The secessionists, who were preparing to take possession of the property of the government in that department and turn the guns of Alcatraz, Fort Point and the Presidio upon the loyalists, were taken completely aback; they delayed action. General Sumner took all precautions against surprise, and the Union men of the Pacific States breathed free again, for civil war had been driven from their doors. Many of the secession leaders, with General Joe Johnston, seeing their plans miscarry, left the State shortly after, and did service in the Confederate armies.

On the steamer from the States that brought the news to California of the disaster at Bull Run, came orders from President Lincoln for that State to furish its quota of men for the Union army The same afternoon, the Franklin Light Infantry, a militia company, composed of printers only, held a meeting at its armory on Sacramento street, and voted unanimously to offer their services to the government, which was accordingly done, and they were the first company that was mustered into the United States service in California, and was afterwards known as Company B, First Infantry, California Volunteers, and were officered as follows : Captain, Valentine Drescher; First Lieutenant, Francis S. Mitchell; Second Lieutenant, George H. Pettis. Other companies were soon formed, and the regiment, with nine companies, went into camp of instruction at Camp Downey, near Oakland.

The regiment had been in camp but a few days when it was ordered to proceed by steamer to Los Angeles, in Southern California. The transfer was made, and the regiment went into camp about nine miles from Los Angeles, on the seashore, where the town of Santa Monica now is. The First Battalion Cavalry, California Volunteers, consisting of five companies, under command of Lieutenant Colonel Davis, who was afterwards killed before Richmond, also accompanied us. In a few days after the establishment of this camp, Lieutenant Pettis, of Company B, was sent on detached duty as recruiting officer to San Francisco, in order that the nine companies now in camp should be filled to the maximum standard. The tenth company had not been admitted to the regiment as yet, although several had made application for the position.

Lieutenant Pettis arrived in San Francisco about the fifteenth of October, and immediately commenced business by opening his recruiting office on the corner of Montgomery and Clay streets, in the same building with the *Morning Call.* He was successful, as by the fifteenth of January he had recruited and sent to the regiment one hundred and two men, and was ordered by General George Wright, then commanding the department of California (and who was afterwards lost on the steamer "Brother Jonathan" on his way to Oregon), to close his office and join his regiment at Camp Latham. In the meantime, four companies of the regiment, under Major E. A. Rigg, had proceeded to Fort Yuma, on the Colorado river, and relieved the regulars who were there. Captain Winfield Scott Hancock, Assistant

Quartermaster United States Army, had also been relieved and ordered to the States. He had been on duty at Los Angeles. Three companies of the regiment had been ordered to Warner's Ranch, about half way between Los Angeles and Fort Yuma, and established Camp Wright. On the twelfth of February, orders had been received by Colonel J. H. Carleton, commanding the regiment, to form the tenth company of his regiment from the recruits enlisted in San Francisco by Lieutenant Pettis. Company K, First Infantry, California Volunteers, was thus formed, and was officered as follows: Captain, Nicholas S. Davis, promoted from First Lieutenant of Company A; First Lieutenant, George H. Pettis, promoted from Second Lieutenant of Company B; Second Lieutenant, Jeremiah Phelan, appointed from Hospital Steward of the regular army.

In the meantime, the government at Washington had received information that General H. H. Sibley had left San Antonio, Texas, with about three thousand seven hundred rebel soldiers for New Mexico, and as the government had immense stores of clothing, camp and garrison equipage, and commissary stores in different posts in that Territory and Arizona, with but few troops to defend them, and a majority of the officers avowed secessionists, the rebels expected an easy conquest. Accordingly, Colonel Carleton had orders to organize what was known as the "California Column," which consisted of the First and Fifth Infantry, California Volunteers, (George W. Bowie was Colonel of the Fifth Infantry, California Volunteers); First Battalion Cavalry, California Volunteers; Company B, Captain John C. Cremoney, Second Cavalry, California Volunteers, and Light Battery A, Third United States Artillery, Captain John B. Shinn.

That an idea may be obtained of the difficulties of this enterprise, I will say that it is about nine hundred miles from Los Angeles to the Rio Grande, not a pound of food or of forage was to be obtained on the route, and everything to be consumed had to be brought from California. Neither was there, as we afterwards ascertained, a single resident in all that long march, except at Fort Yuma. The country through which the "Column" passed was without water, and the Colorado and Gila Deserts to be

crossed before we should come in sight of the green
cottonwoods of the Rio Grande. The Apache
Indians supposed that they had driven all the whites
out of the Territory of Arizona, and the former required constant watching and attention. In conse-
quence of the scarcity of water on the route, the
" Column " could only be moved in detachments.

Companies K and C, First Infantry, and Company
G, Fifth Infantry, Captain Hugh L. Hinds, left
Captain Latham about the first of March, 1862,
under command of Captain William McMullen, of
Company C, and arrived at Camp Wright in due
season, it being about one hundred and forty miles.
The only incident on this march worthy of mention
was, that when the battalion marched through the
town of Los Angeles the American flag had been
hauled down from the court house. As it was well
known that the people of Los Angeles at that time
were nearly all strong in their sympathies with the
rebellion, it was thought that the hauling down of the
flag was to insult the command. Consequently, on
the arrival of the battalion on the banks of the Los
Angeles river, which flows on the eastern side of the

town, it was halted and Captain McMullen returned, and, finding some of the town officials, insisted that the flag should be hoisted immediately. The citizens denied any intended insult to the flag, and proceeded to replace it, which being seen by the men of the battalion, they gave three cheers, and continued on their way.

A delay of a couple of weeks at Camp Wright, when orders were received by Lieutenant Colonel J. R. West, of the First Infantry, commanding at Camp Wright, to organize the advance detachment of the " Column," to consist of Companies K and C, First Infantry, California Volunteers, and Companies B and G, Fifth Infantry, California Volunteers, and proceed without delay to Fort Yuma. The command as above constituted left camp at a late hour in the afternoon, and after a short march made camp beside a laguna, or pond. It rained during the night, and daylight found us at breakfast, which was quickly dispatched, and we were soon on our march, the road continually ascending. At nine o'clock in the forenoon we had reached the line of snow, where

2

it was snowing heavily. At noon we had reached the summit, and found the snow about two feet in depth, and as cold as Greenland. A short halt was made, when great fires were built to warm the men, and then the command moved down the mountain. At three o'clock in the afternoon we passed through the line of snow, shortly after through the precipitous cañon of San Felipe, and towards evening went into camp, the grass being more than knee high, the air redolent with the perfume of flowers and the sweet melody of the birds.

A short march the next day brought us to Las Dos Palmas, or the "Two Palms," so called from the fact that two luxuriant palm trees formerly flourished here, the stumps of which were then to be seen. Thence to Carizo Creek, nine miles, where the command rested one day. Here commences the then much-dreaded Colorado Desert. For more than a hundred miles we were at the mercy of its sands and storms and burning sun. Such another scene of desolation does not exist on the American continent; treeless mountains on either side, brown and sombre to their very tops; no signs of life were to be seen anywhere. Although it was in the first days of April, still the sun poured down with an intensity that I had never before experienced, no shade could be found, and the very water in the creek could not be bathed in—being more fit for cooking than bathing, it being so hot. Such was the Colorado Desert as we approached it. What will it be further on? We shall see.

The command left camp at Carizo Creek in the middle of the afternoon, and continued the march until midnight, when we arrived at Sackett's Wells. Here it was supposed a ration of water for the men would be found, but upon examination it was ascertained that somebody had knocked the bottom out of the well, and no water was to be obtained, except such as could be caught in cups as it trickled drop by drop from the strata of clay that had heretofore formed the bottom of the well. No camp could be made here, and the command moved on, marching until about ten o'clock in the morning, when we arrived at the Indian Wells, having made thirty-two miles. A large number of the men were now suffering for the want of water, and the animals, upon discovering the green bushes in the distance, near these wells, pricked their ears, and every exertion was required by riders and drivers to prevent a stampede, so much were they in want of water. Upon our arrival it was found that but a few buckets of water was in the well, as a detachment of cavalry had made camp there the day before, and had only left upon seeing our command approach, using all the water in the well for their animals before leaving. However, guards were placed over the well, men sent down to pass the water up as it collected, and in the course of a few hours the men had each received his pint of water; then the animals were furnished.

Before the water had all been distributed, one of those terrible sand storms for which this desert is renowned began, and as the sun went down it was at its very height. Neither man nor animal could face this shower of stones and gravel, and the sand and dust penetrated everything. The only thing that was to be done was to throw oneself down upon his face, draw his blankets around him, and ride it out, sleeping. The storm continued through the night, and before dawn approached it had ceased, and upon crawling out of my sand bank, I saw in all directions what appeared to be graves, but they were only mounds of sand that had been formed by the storm over the bodies of the soldiers. Imagine, if you can, near four hundred of these mounds becoming animate and dissolving in the desert, as reveille sounded.

At about noon the command moved on, and after marching twenty-five miles arrived at Alamo Mucho at about two o'clock in the morning. Here was found a well that would have furnished water for an army corps — sweet, cold water. It was a pleasure to look at this, to hold it in a tin cup, look at it, take a mouthful, holding it there a time before swallowing it; it seemed a sin to drink it. This water was not taken on the point of the bayonet, as water had been taken for the past four days, and we had marched sixty-six miles from Los Dos Palmos since we had our fill of water. After the men had satisfied their thirst they spread their blankets wherever they pleased, and there was no person in that command, except the guard, that was not soon in the arms of Morpheus.

Before daylight another sand storm commenced, and when reveille was beat off, not a dozen men were in line, and they were only brought out of their sand hills by beating the long roll. The storm subsided in the early afternoon, when the command moved on, making Gardiner's Wells, twelve miles, before sundown, where was found a fine well with plenty of water, but none of the command wanted any, the only objection being, and that a slight one, that there was standing above the level of the water in the well, a pair of boots—and a dead man in them. Seven Wells was soon reached, and, as the name implies, there were plenty of wells, but there was no water. Thence to Cook's Well, twelve miles, with plenty of good water, thence fourteen miles to the Colorado river, at Algodones. The next day, before noon, the command arrived at Fort Yuma and went into camp. Here we met Don Pascual, a head chief of the Yumas, Don Diego Jaeger, and the "Great Western," three of the most celebrated characters in the annals of Fort Yuma.

It was supposed that our command was to constitute the advance of the "Column" from Fort Yuma.

But upon our arrival at that point, we found that a reconnoitering party, consisting of Company I, First California Infantry, Captain W. P. Calloway; Company A, First California Cavalry, Captain William McLeave, and Lieutenant Phelan, with detachments for two mountain howitzers, had been sent up the Gila river, as the Indians had reported that a large body of rebels were advancing on Fort Yuma from Tucson. On the third day after our arrival we crossed over the Colorado river and continued our march. We passed the divide between the Colorado and Gila rivers, and arrived at Gila City that afternoon, eighteen miles. Our route was the old overland stage route on the south side of the Gila. Here we first saw that peculiar and picturesque cactus, so characteristic of the country, called by the Indians "*petayah*," but more generally known as the "*suaro*," and recognized by botanists as the "*Cereus grandeus.*"

Our next march was to Filibuster camp, eleven miles; thence to Antelope Peak, fifteen; Mohawk, twelve; Texas Hill, eleven; Stanwix, seventeen; Burke's, twelve miles. Here we found the reconnoitering party, under Captain Calloway, that had

left Fort Yuma a few days before our arrival there.
They had had a brush with the rebels at Picacho,
a point about forty-five miles west of Tucson. Lieutenant Barrett, Company A, First Cavalry, California Volunteers, and three men of the same company,
had been killed. They had secured three rebel
prisoners. The poor devils were under guard beneath
some cottonwoods in their camp. They were now
on their return to Fort Yuma.

The next morning our command moved out with
more alacrity than usual, for we felt that we were
now the advance of the " Column," and we would
meet the rebels, too. A short march of twelve
miles brought us to Oatman Flat. We had come
down from the high mesa lands into this valley, and
as we passed through near the middle of it, saw upon
the right side of the road a small enclosure of rails,
on one end of which was inscribed " The Oatman
Family." We had all heard of this tragedy years
before, and now we were upon the spot where the
terrible massacre had been perpetrated. No one of
us could look upon this humble monument without
awakening a feeling of revenge, and many were the

silent pledges given that day that when the oppor-
tunity should offer, that at least one shot would be
given for these silent victims to Indian treachery.
One officer was so affected that he approached Colonel J. R. West, our commanding officer, with the
interrogatory : "Colonel, if we should at any time
meet any of these Indians, what course should be
pursued towards them?" "Tell your men when
they see a head, hit it if they can!" was the Colonel's quick rejoinder. You may think this to have
been rather harsh, but remember we were standing
above the remains of the innocent victims of a most
terrible tragedy.

A few miles after leaving Oatman's Flat we came
to a pile of immense boulders in the centre of a
pleasant valley. These were the famous "Pedras
Pintados," or painted rocks. A march of fourteen
miles brought the command to Kenyon's. The next
day, after sixteen miles marching, we arrived at
Gila Bend. Here we lay over a day, as our next
march was to be to the Maricopa Wells, forty miles
distant, the dreaded Gila Desert. After marching
all night and all of the next day, we approached the

Maricopa Wells at about twelve o'clock on the second night. When within a mile of this point, a small reconnoitering party that had been sent ahead of our command, met us and reported that a large force of the rebels had possession of the wells, and from appearances intended to prevent our command from reaching there. This report served to put new life into everybody, notwithstanding that the whole command had now been without sleep for over forty hours, had marched forty miles and was somewhat fatigued. One company was thrown out as skirmishers, the rest of the command in line of battle. We approached the watering place, and when we arrived there, instead of finding a formidable enemy, we found a half a dozen of our own cavalry that had been scouting ahead of the command. We found the water strongly impregnated with alkali, but it served to assuage our thirst.

A short march of ten miles then brought us to the Casa Blanca, the largest village of the Pimo Indians. Our command remained here for several weeks, until at least a large part of the "Column" had arrived, and large stores of commissaries and forage had been collected. Our Indian scouts and spies brought every few days extravagant reports of the force of rebels at Tucson, and they all agreed that when our troops should reach that point, we would meet with a warm reception, and that rifle-pits, sufficiently manned, extended a long ways on either side of the town. These Indians were on the best of terms with us, as they had sold large amounts of their produce to our command, for which they had been promptly and abundantly paid—a different experience when the rebels were there. They had been employed by our quartermaster's department as herders of our beef cattle, and were paid to their own satisfaction for all services they had rendered, but no inducement that our commander offered them, no amount of pay, could influence any one of them to accompany us towards Tucson, so assured were they that we were to be "wiped out" before we should reach there.

On or about the twelfth day of May, 1862, the advance, constituted as before stated, with B Company, California Cavalry, Captain Emil Fritz, added, left the peaceful and hospitable homes of the Pimos, and arrived at the Sacatone, twelve miles. Here we left the overland mail road, which we had followed since leaving Los Angeles, and keeping up the south bank of the Gila to White's Ranch; thence to the celebrated ruins of the Casa Blanca, so graphically described by Mr. John R. Bartlett in his "Personal Narratives" of the Boundary Commission; thence to Rattlesnake Spring; thence to old Fort Breckenridge, which had been so cowardly deserted the year before by our regular troops; thence to Cañon de Oro. As we now approached Tucson, everything was in fighting trim. A short halt was made near the town, and the cavalry company, in two divisions, approached the place from the north and west. The infantry marched in by the main street from the west, with the field music playing "Yankee Doodle," and instead of being received by shot and shell, we found neither friend nor enemy, only a village without population, if we except some hundreds of dogs and cats.

When we were at the Pimos, Governor Pesquira, of Sonora, Mexico, arrived there from California on his way home; he was allowed to pass our lines; he and his party arrived in Tucson a few days before our command, and found the place nearly deserted. Captain Hunter, with his rebel soldiers, were far on their way to the Rio Grande, and as they had assured the native population — wholly Mexican — that when the "Abs"—meaning the Union troops — arrived they would massacre all the men and abuse all the women, they stood not upon the order of going, but went at once for Sonora. Governor Pesquira hurried forward, overtaking parties of the fugitives each day, and assuring them of different treatment from the Union soldiers than they had been told by the rebels, induced many to return to their homes, and within a week Tucson was again alive; stores and gambling saloons were numerous, the military had taken possession of the best buildings in the town for quarters, and the stars and stripes again waved over the Capital of the Territory of Arizona.

The advance of the "Column" entered Tucson on the twentieth day of May, 1862. Several Americans, among them Sylvester Mowry, formerly of

3

Rhode Island, returned, and being violent in their sympathies with the rebellion, were arrested. Some were sent out of the Territory, while Mowry was sent to Fort Yuma, where he remained incarcerated a long time. About the fifteenth of June, Captain N. S. Davis was relieved from the command of Company K by Lieutenant Pettis, who remained in command, with a short interval, until its final muster out. Captain Davis was on duty in the quartermaster's department. By the first of July, a large part of the "Column" had arrived at Tucson, a large depot of army stores had been brought from California, and preparations were commenced for the movement again of the advance column. Several spies and scouts had been sent forward from Tucson, but as they had not returned, matters were rather uncertain. However, in the first week in July, Company E, First California Infantry, Captain Thomas L. Roberts, and Company B, Second California Cavalry, were ordered to proceed to Apache Pass and hold possession of the water at that point. On the twentieth of July the advance column left Tucson, and on the second day arrived at the San Pedro, twenty-five miles. Here a delay of one day was made to put the fording place in good order for the crossing of the "Column." Information was received here that Captain Roberts' advance into the Apache Pass had been attacked by a large force of the Apaches, under the renowned chief, "Cochise," and after fighting during an entire afternoon had succeeded in driving the Indians, with a loss on our side of several of our men killed and wounded.

Our next march was to Dragoon Springs, eighteen miles; thence to Sulphur Springs, twenty-two miles. The famous Apache Pass was reached by another march of twenty-five miles. Here was found the command of Captain Roberts, with evidences of the struggle of a few days before. On leaving Apache Pass the next day, we were again the advance of the "Column," which position was retained until our arrival on the Rio Grande. The next camping ground was at San Simon, eighteen miles. As we were assured by our guides that no water would be found until we reached *Ojo de Vaca*, or Cow Springs, a distance of sixty-seven miles, it was deemed advisable to leave the overland route at this point, and

proceed by another route. Accordingly, the next
morning the command moved south, following up the
San Simon Valley, a distance of twelve miles, and
camped at the Cienega. Here was found water, the
best and most abundant on the whole march. Imagine, if you can, a valley twenty miles in width, on
either side a range of mountains; and to the north
and south, up and down the valley, a level plain as
far as the eye could reach. A trench three feet
wide, by five or six in depth, filled nearly to the top
with clear cold water, running with a velocity of at
least six miles an hour, the bottom covered with
white smooth pebbles. Two miles above this point
no water was to be found. As you descended the
valley and approached this water, you found at first
the ground moist, then water appeared, a mere drop,
then a small stream of running water, which increased
in volume, until you found a stream as described
above. Below this point the water gradually les-
sened, until, two miles below, this magnificent stream
had entirely disappeared. There was no shade to
be had here, except that found under the wagon
bodies, still there was no fault found; the fine stream

of water that we were enjoying satisfied us for all other discomforts. It was with feelings of regret that we left this point late the next afternoon, with well filled canteens; and the uncertainty of finding water in advance, added to this feeling. We arrived at Leiteresdorffer's Wells soon after sunset, but no water was to be found. The march was continued during the night, and all of the next day, until we arrived at Soldier's Farewell, and no water. The command was strung out a distance of at least five miles; we had been marching thirty hours, with only a canteen each of water, with the thermometer at least 130. A large number of the men had given out and were scattered in parties of three or four, for a dozen miles in the rear. What was left of the command moved on, and after leaving the wagon road, we arrived in Burro Cañon, some time after dark, where plenty of water was found, when, after taking in a fill, turned into our blankets, entirely forgetting our hunger in our weariness. Company K marched into Burro Cañon with less than ten men out of eighty, and it was long after daylight the next day before the whole command had arrived. A

short march of twelve miles brought us to Ojo de
Baca ; thence eighteen miles to the Miembres river.

Our next march, twenty-five miles, was to Cooke's
Springs, passing through Cooke's Cañon.   This
location was known by Mexicans as *La Valle del
Muerto*, or Valley of Death.   It seemed to be
rightly named, too, as for nearly two miles were to
be seen, on either side, skulls and other portions of
human remains who had fallen by Indian assassina-
tion.   Mounds and crosses were met every few
minutes.   As we emerged from this *triste* locality,
we encountered the remains of wagons and government stores, that had been destroyed the year before
by the regular troops, who had deserted Forts Bu-
chanan and Breckenridge, in Arizona.   When they
had arrived at this point, they were informed of the
surrender of the regulars at Fort Fillmore ; consequently, without further inquiry, they destroyed all
the government property they had in charge, and
made their way, on the west side of the Rio Grande,
to Fort Craig.

The next march brought us near to Mule Springs,
fifteen miles ; and on the next afternoon could be

discovered, in the distance, the green, winding way of the Rio Grande, with the Sierras de Organos in the background. Camp was made that night on the banks of the Rio Bravo del Norte, near to old Fort Thorn. The next march was down the west bank of the river to the fording place, known as San Diego, which you will find set down on all maps as a town or village, but to my certain knowledge, up to the time mentioned, and for several years afterwards, there was but one house in the vicinity, and that contained but one room and no roof. As the river was now, the third of August, at its extreme height, caused by the melting of the snow in the upper Rocky Mountains, we experienced some difficulty in getting our wagons and stores across; still all was completed before sundown, and the next day we arrived at Roblado, near the town of Dona Ana. On the fifth of August, after passing through the villages of Dona Ana and Las Cruces, we arrived at the pleasant town of La Mesilla.

Here was to be our resting place. We found a well-built village, with a numerous population, mostly Mexican. The rebels, who had arrived in the Territory, we learned, had, after the treacherous surrender of the regular troops at Fort Fillmore (directly opposite La Mesilla), marched north. They found Fort Craig too strong to be attacked, and, contrary to all military maxims, had continued on, leaving a fortified position in their rear. The desperate battle of Val Verde had taken place on the twenty-first and twenty-second of February, 1862, a short distance above Fort Craig. And as long as Major Benny Roberts had command of the Federal troops they were successful, but when General E. R. S. Canby came on the field and took command, the rebels soon had turned the tide of the battle in their favor. McRae's battery was taken, and our troops were returning, panic-stricken, across the river, and fleeing towards Fort Craig, about three miles down the river. The rebels then approached Albuquerque, where was stored a large amount of government stores, which were surrendered without a struggle. Thence they proceeded to Santa Fé, where, without opposition, they took possession. There was one other fort to be taken, about one hundred miles northwest — Fort Union. After some delay at Santa Fé, the rebels, numbering some sixteen hundred, set out for Fort Union. At Apache Pass, or Pigeon's Ranch, they were met by a Colorado regiment, with what regulars and militia could be found, all under command of Colonel John P Slough (afterwards chief justice of the Territory), and were defeated, their wagons, ammunition, and all their stores having been destroyed by a party of Union troops under Captain W. H. Lewis, Fifth United States Infantry, and Captain A. B. Cary, of the Third United States Infantry, who scaled a mountain and got into their rear. The rebels precipitately retreated from this point, to and down the Rio Grande, having passed La Mesilla a few weeks before our arrival, and left the Territory with about twelve hundred men out of thirty-seven hundred, that they had arrived with.

The different companies of the "Column," as they arrived, were now sent to different points in the department. Our Colonel, James H. Carleton, had been promoted to Brigadier General, and had relieved General E. R. S. Canby, in command of the department of New Mexico. The regular troops were all relieved, except the Fifth Infantry, and sent east, and a protection was now assured to the population, by the California Volunteers.   Lieutenant Colonel J. R. West was now promoted to Colonel of the regiment, and in command of the southern district of the department.   Fine quarters were found for the command in the village of La Mesilla, and the district was under martial law.   Duty was really pleasant here, — plenty of society, with frequent *bailes*, few drills, and plenty of everything to eat and drink. The white population were nearly all of secession proclivities, one in particular, Samuel L. Jones (better known as the pro-slavery Sheriff Jones, of Kansas), who resided here, was arrested usually about once a week, and incarcerated in the guard-house for treasonable utterances.

After a protracted season of this duty, or up to about the twentieth of November, came the most unpleasant part of the history of Company K.   There had been several escapes from the guard-house of persons who had been imprisoned for treasonable utterances, until it seemed that there might exist a disposition among some of the command to be a party to these frequent escapades. This state of affairs existed until one morning an escape was reported to the commanding officer, Colonel West, who immediately ordered the sergeant of the guard, with sentinels numbers one, two, three, four and five, who were on duty at the time, to be placed in the guard-house, in irons. It so happened that this sergeant and all the sentinels belonged to Company K, and at the morning drill, after guard mount, the company refused to do further duty, or until the irons were taken off of Sergeant Miller. The soldier most aggrieved appeared to be Corporal Charles Smith, or rather he acted as spokesman for the company. The company was immediately ordered into their quarters by Lieutenant Pettis, and put under guard, and the facts reported to the commanding officer. Orders were given for all prisoners to be placed in the guard-house; Company K was ordered to proceed to the plaza or parade without arms, when the long roll was beat. The other two companies of the garrison were soon on the plaza, fully equipped. Colonel West now made his appearance, mounted; he then marched Company A, Fifth California Infantry, about five paces in front of and facing Company K, with pieces loaded, and at a "ready." He then called Corporal Smith to the front, and asked him if he still persisted in refusing to do his duty? The Corporal respectfully, but firmly, announced that he would do no duty until the irons were removed from Sergeant Miller. Company D, First California Infantry, had been wheeled to the right out of line, and the Corporal was now ordered to place himself about six paces in front of this company Upon his again refusing to do duty, Captain Mitchell, of Company D, was ordered to fire upon him. This order was unhesitatingly obeyed; and after the smoke had cleared away, it was seen that the Corporal was uninjured. Not so with some others. The position of Company D was such that it was facing the cathedral, which is situated on the west side of the plaza; on either side of the cathedral were long straight streets, running from the plaza; the long roll and the other preparations had called all the inhabitants from their residences, and the result of the first volley was to wound two invalid soldiers, together with one Mexican woman and one child, and the cathedral, which was built of adobes, was concealed for a few minutes by its own dust, caused by the minie balls penetrating its front. The Corporal was again questioned by Colonel West, who returned his former answer, and Company D again fired a volley, but the Corporal remained untouched. After another questioning by the Colonel, Company D was once more ordered to fire, when, between the commands " aim," " fire," Colonel West rode up behind the company with uplifted sabre, and gave the command to " lower those rifles," when the command was given by the Captain to " fire." At this discharge, the Corporal fell to the ground, a minie ball having passed directly through him, having entered his right breast. He was immediately placed upon a stretcher, and expired on his way to the hospital. The rest of the company was now questioned by Colonel West, and each man asserted his willingness to do his duty, when the command was dismissed to their quarters, and Company K immediately assumed their arms and accoutrements and appeared upon the plaza for drill. This was

4

the only evidence of insubordination ever shown in
the " Column," and the prompt manner in which this
one was met and punished, precluded any danger of
another exhibition of this character.

A few days after these occurrences, some of our
spies and scouts brought in the intelligence that
another large party of rebels had left San Antonio,
Texas, for New Mexico. Accordingly, Companies
K and D were ordered to San Elizario, Texas, a
town about twenty-five miles below El Paso, Mexico,
and the last point of civilization towards San
Antonio, on outpost duty After remaining here
about six weeks, and no rebels appearing, Company
K was ordered to Fort Craig. A march of twenty-
five miles brought us to Franklin or Fort Bliss,
directly opposite El Paso; thence two marches,
aggregating fifty miles, found us in our old quarters
at La Mesilla, where the company was ordered to
remain until the adjournment of a general court-
martial which was then in session at that post. A
week later, and Company K commenced its march
for Fort Craig. A short march brought us again to
Dona Ana. Three miles from that village brought

us to the commencement of the much dreaded
Jornada del Muerto (Journey of Death). The
Jornada is a large desert, well supplied with fine
gramma grass in some portions, but absolutely desti-
tue of water or shade for seventy-five miles. Why
it ever received its title, I never distinctly learned,
but suppose it was on account of the very numerous
massacres committed on it by the Apache Indians.
On the east, in the far distance, are the Sierras
Blancos, and is fringed on the west by the Sierra
Caballo and Sierra de Frey Cristobal. From these
heights, on either side, the Indians are enabled to distinctly perceive any party of travellers coming over
the wide and unsheltered expanse of the *Jornada
del Muerto*. When any such parties are seen, they
come sweeping down upon the unsuspecting immigrant in more than usual numbers, and if successful,
as they generally are, in their attack, invariably
destroy all of the party, for there is no possible
chance of escape; and the Apaches never take any
prisoners but women and young children, and they
become captives for life.

The first camp was a dry one, and as the com-

mand was accompanied by a tank of water, drawn
by six mules, thus being prepared by a plentiful
supply of water, I concluded to cross this desert at
my leisure. The next forenoon we passed by the
celebrated "Point of Rocks," the company being
deployed as skirmishers, with the hope of finding
Indians hiding between the huge boulders of which
it was composed, but without results. Late in the
afternoon we arrived at the Aleman, so called from
the fact that a whole German immigrant family had
been massacred at this point some years before by
the Indians. The next night another dry camp,
having passed during the day the *Laguna del Muerto*,
where water is found in some seasons. While some
three miles on our left was the *Ojo del Muerto*, a
point where Fort McRae was established in 1863 by
Captain Henry A. Greene, commanding Company
G, First California Infantry, now a resident of this
city, (Providence, R. I.) The next day's march
brought us to the little village of El Paraje del Fra
Cristobal. Near the spot on which the camp was
made, was the peaceful flowing and muddy Rio
Grande. A short march of five miles brought us to

our destination — Fort Craig. Our arrival was in January, 1863.

The company remained at this post during the year 1863, monotony of garrison life being relieved by furnishing escorts to wagon trains bound north and south, and an occasional scout after Indians. In July of that year, Assistant Surgeon Watson, who had been commissioned at Sacramento, California, more than a year before, and had been ordered to report to the headquarters of his regiment at Fort Craig, arrived at Fort McRae, without accident. On leaving that post, Captain Greene had furnished him with one government wagon and an escort of five or six men of his company. They set out with joyful anticipation; the Doctor was delighted to know that after a year's travel, he would soon be at his new home, and be doing duty with his own regiment, which he had never seen. The wagon, with its occupants, soon emerged from the cañon of the *Ojo del Muerto*, and came out on the hard, smooth, natural road of the *Jornada*. About the middle of the afternoon, they were proceeding leisurely along; twelve miles in advance could be plainly seen the buildings

of Fort Craig, with "Old Glory" on the flag-staff.
The driver of the team, Johnson, a soldier of Greene's
company, sat on his near wheel-mule chatting pleas-
antly with the Doctor, who occupied the front of the
wagon, with his feet hanging down on the whiffle-
trees; the escort were all in the wagon, lying on
their blankets, with their arms and equipments
beneath them. Within five miles of them there was
not a rock, tree, shrub, or bush, as large as a man's
head — they felt a perfect security Another mo-
ment, how changed! There arose from the sand of
the desert, where they had buried themselves, some
ten or twelve Apaches, within twenty feet of the
moving wagon, and poured a volley of arrows into
the doomed party, and closing in immediately, a
part attacked the occupants of the wagon, while the
rest disengaged the mules, and mounting their backs
started for the mountains on the west, towards the
river, and before the soldiers were out of the wagon
were out of reach of their fire. Doctor Watson was
shot with two arrows, one in his right arm, and the
other on the inside of his right thigh, severing the
femoral artery He breathed his last in a few min-

utes; the driver was shot through the heart, and one or two of the escorts were slightly wounded. News of this affair reached the post before sunset, and in twenty minutes Company K was on its way down the west side of the river to intercept, if possible, these murderers. The company was kept in the field for thirty days, without other result than to find a hot trail of eighty-two Navajoes, who were on their way to their own country, with some eight thousand head of sheep and other stock that they had stolen in the upper counties of New Mexico. As the company were dismounted, it was impossible to take up the trail. The commander of the company, however, with five cavalrymen and two Mexican scouts, followed and overtook the Indians after a run of twenty-five miles, but accomplished nothing except exchanging some twenty or twenty-five shots on either side, as our animals were completely "blown," and eighty-two to eight was an unpleasant disparity of numbers. The lieutenant and his men arrived back at the river the next morning, having been in the saddle nearly twenty-four hours. The result of the short skirmish was that one of the cavalrymen's horses was shot through the breast, and one Navajo was sent to his happy hunting-grounds and one was wounded.

January, 1864, Company K was ordered to Los Pinos, about one hundred miles further up the Rio Grande, and about twenty miles south of Albuquerque; marching through the towns of Socoreo, La Limitar, across the sand hills at the foot of the *Sierra de los Ladrones*, or Thieves Mountains; crossing the Rio Puerco, near its affluence with the Rio Grande; thence to Sabinal, La Belen, and Los Lunes. They remained here until the first of February, when Colonel Kit Carson arrived there from the Navajo country, with some two hundred and fifty-three Navajo Indians, whom he had taken prisoners in his operations against that nation. Orders were received from department headquarters for Company K to proceed with these Indians to the Bosque Redonde, some two hundred and fifty miles down on the Pecos river. Accordingly, after formally receiving these prisoners and receipting therefor, the command moved out, and on the second night arrived at Carnwell Cañon; thence to San Antonio, San Antoinette,

Los Placeres and Gallisteo. Thus far the command had moved across the country, but on the day of leaving Gallisteo, the company struck the military road leading from Fort Union to Santa Fé, near the old Peces ruins. The command moved along this road to the village of Tecolote; from here they proceeded down the Pecos river, and arrived at Fort Sumner after eighteen days' marching. Fort Sumner was a new post, established for the purpose of a reservation for Indians, both Navajo and Apache, that should be taken prisoners by the troops, and Colonel Carson was on a campaign against the Navajos, in which he was successful, as there were finally some eight thousand of these Indians captured and placed on this reservation. Those brought in by Company K were the first large body that had arrived. I will say here, in parenthesis, that this is the only way to treat the Indian question; for this Indian nation (the Navajoes), after receiving a severe drubbing by Carson, and all had surrendered, were finally allowed to return to their own country, since which time they have continued on the best of terms with our people. This has always been the experience on the frontiers — one effective campaign is better than all the treaties that were ever consummated.

Fort Sumner was at this time in command of Major Henry D. Wallen, United States Seventh Infantry, than whom there was no more excellent gentleman in the service of the government. His administration was marked by a sincere desire to do justice to all under him, a feature that was sadly deficient in too many officers of the time that is spoken of. He was a perfect example of sobriety, and his case certainly was a commendation of the excellence of education of the academy at West Point, of which he was an honored graduate.

Company K had been at Fort Sumner but a few days when it was ordered to report to the commanding officer at Fort Union, necessitating a march of one hundred and twenty-five miles. The command arrived at Fort Union on the eighteenth day of March, 1864, and remained there, doing camp duty, during the months of April, May and June. In July, the company proceeded, with a company of New Mexican cavalry, towards the east, by the

route known as the Cummarron route, passing on
our way, Burgwin's Spring, named after the gallant
Captain Burgwin, First Regiment United States
Dragoons, who fell while leading the attack upon the
insurgents at Taos, 1847, and the Wagon Mound, a
high landmark (so called from its shape). From
this point to the "Point of Rocks," forty miles, is
the track of a bloody, brave and disastrous fight
made by eight passengers in the stage against a band
of sixty Apaches. They fought every inch of the
long, dread struggle. Killed one by one, and
dropped on the road, two survivors maintained their
defense a long time, and when the sole contestant
was left, his last dying effort was to strew the con-
tents of his powder-horn in the sand, and stir it in
with his foot, so that the Indians could not use it.
Wilson's Creek, some miles further on, is named
after a Mr. Wilson, a merchant of Santa Fé, who
was overtaken here by the Indians, and, with his
wife and child — for he was alone with them —
butchered with the usual savage outrage and cruelty

The command returned to Fort Union in Septem-
ber, in which month the First Infantry, California

Volunteers, was mustered out of service, their term
of three years having expired, with the exception of
Company K, it being recollected that they were enlisted at San Francisco some time after the other
companies had been formed. However, the mem-
bers of that company began, in October, to be
dropped out, and when orders arrived at Fort Union
for the formation of the Commanche expedition,
under Colonel Kit Carson, there remained of the
First Infantry Regiment, California Volunteers, one
officer (Lieutenant Pettis) and twenty-six enlisted
men of Company K.   This company accompanied
Carson's expedition with two mountain howitzers,
mounted on prairie carriages, and rendezvoued at
Fort Bascom, on the Canadian river, near the line of
Texas.   This expedition consisted as follows : Colonel Christopher Carson, First New Mexico Cavalry,
commanding ; Colonel Francisco P Abreú, First
New Mexico Infantry ; Major William McCleave,
First California Cavalry ; Captain Emil Fritz, Company B, First California Cavalry. one officer and
forty enlisted men ; Lieutenant Sullivan Heath,
Company K, First California Cavalry, one officer and

forty men; Captain Meriam, Company M, First California Cavalry, one officer and thirty-four men; Lieutenant George H. Pettis, Company K, First California Infantry, one officer and twenty-six men; Captain Charles Deus, Company M, First New Mexico Cavalry, two officers and seventy men; Captain Joseph Berney, Company D, First New Mexico Cavalry, two officers and thirty-six men; Company A, First California Veteran Infantry, seventy-five men; Assistant Surgeon George S. Courtright, United States Volunteers, and an officer whose name escapes me, as Assistant Quartermaster and Commissary, — numbering in all, fourteen officers and three hundred and twenty-one enlisted men. In addition to the command, Colonel Carson had induced seventy-two friendly Indians (Utes and Apaches), and as big scoundrels as there were on the frontiers, by promising them all the plunder that they might acquire, to join the expedition.

On the sixth of November, the command left Fort Bascom, and proceeded down on the north bank of the Canadian, hoping to find the Commanche and

Kiowa Indians (who had been committing their
atrocities during the whole of 1864) in their winter
quarters. The Indians with our command, on every
night, after making camp, being now on the war-
path, indulged in the accustomed war dance, which,
although new to most of us, became almost intoler-
able, it being kept up each night until nearly day-
break; and until we became accustomed to their
groans and howlings, incident to the dance, it was
impossible to sleep. Each morning of our march,
two of our Indians would be sent ahead several hours
before we started, who would return to camp at night
and report.

We had been on our march day after day without
particular incident until our arrival at Mule Creek,
when our scouts brought in the intelligence that they
had seen signs of a large body of Indians that had
moved that day, and that they could be overtaken
without much effort. Immediately after supper, all
of the Cavalry, with Company K, moved out of camp
in light marching order, leaving the infantry, under
command of Colonel Abreü, to protect the wagon
train and proceed on our trail on the morrow   Col-

onel Carson and command marched all night, except a short halt just before dawn, and struck an outpost of the enemy on the opposite side of the river, at about sunrise, who being mounted retreated, followed by our Indians and two companies of our Cavalry. The rest of the command moved down on the north side of the river, and a few miles below the cavalry struck a Kiowa *rancheria* of one hundred and seventy-six lodges, the Indians retreating down the river on their approach. Company K, escorted by Lieutenant Heath's command, and accompanied by Colonel Carson, could not advance with the rapidity of the cavalry, as the cannoneers were dismounted, and the wheels tracking very narrow, caused the utmost attention to prevent their being overturned. The Indians from the Kiowa encampment retreated until they were reinforced by a large force of Commanches from a Commanche *rancheria* of five hundred lodges, a short distance below the "Adobe Walls," a location well known by all frontiersmen. The cavalry made a stand here, and were engaged in skirmishing with the enemy, when Company K came on the field with the two mountain howitzers. An order from Colonel

Carson to Lieutenant Pettis to "fling a few shell over thar!" indicating with his hand a large body of Indians who appeared to be about to charge into our forces, that officer immediately ordered "Battery halt! action right, load with shell — load!" Before the fourth discharge of the howitzers, the Indians had retreated out of range, and it was supposed that there would be no more fighting; but we counted without our host, for our animals had scarcely been watered when the enemy returned to the conflict. The horses of the cavalry were again placed in the "Adobe Walls," which were elevated enough to protect them from the rifle balls of the enemy, and the fight was soon at its height.

About the middle of the afternoon, Carson concluded to return to the Kiowa village that we had passed through in the morning, contrary to the wishes of his officers, who were anxious to advance to the Commanche village, which was less than a mile in our front. The return column consisted of the cavalry horses, the number four of each set of fours leading the other three horses, with the howitzers in the rear, the dismounted cavalry acting as skirmishers on the front, rear and either flank. The firing was continued from each side until the village was reached, when our troops proceeded to destroy it, which was effectually done before dark.

A further march of about four miles, and the wagon train was reached, the safety of which had been the subject of much anxiety during the day The gun carriages and ammunition carts of Company K were packed with the wounded on their return from the Kiowa village. A rest was had the next day, which was sadly needed, as the whole command had been marching and fighting about twenty-seven hours, on a few broken hard tack and a slice of salt pork each. The second day after the fight, Carson concluded to return to Fort Bascom, which post was reached in twenty-one days. Here the command remained until orders were received from General Carleton, commanding the department, and Company K was ordered to Fort Union, as the term of service of nearly all the men had expired. By the first of February, 1865, all the enlisted men of the company had been mustered out of service, and Lieutenant Pettis, the last man of his regiment, was ordered to report to the mustering officer at Santa Fé, with all the records of his company ; and on the fifteenth of February, he was mustered out of service, and Company K, First Infantry, California Volunteers, had ceased to exist, having marched on foot during its term of service four thousand two hundred and forty-five miles.